SPIDERS

SPIDERS

by **George Shea**

illustrated by **Scott W. Earle**

EMC Corporation, St. Paul, Minnesota

PHOTO CREDITS

Field Museum of Natural History, Chicago: 10
A. M. Winchester, University of Northern Colorado: 9

Library of Congress Cataloging in Publication Data

Shea, George.
  Spiders.

  (Four (not so) awful creatures)
  SUMMARY: Explains the facts about spiders,
eight-legged creatures useful for insect control
and less dangerous than commonly believed.
  1. Spiders—Juvenile literature. [1. Spiders]
I. Earle, Scott W.   II. Title.   III. Series.
QL458.4.C53   595'.44   77-338
ISBN 0-88436-306-6
ISBN 0-88436-307-4 pbk.

Published by EMC Corporation
180 East Sixth Street
St. Paul, Minnesota 55101
Printed in the United States of America
0 9 8 7 6 5 4 3 2

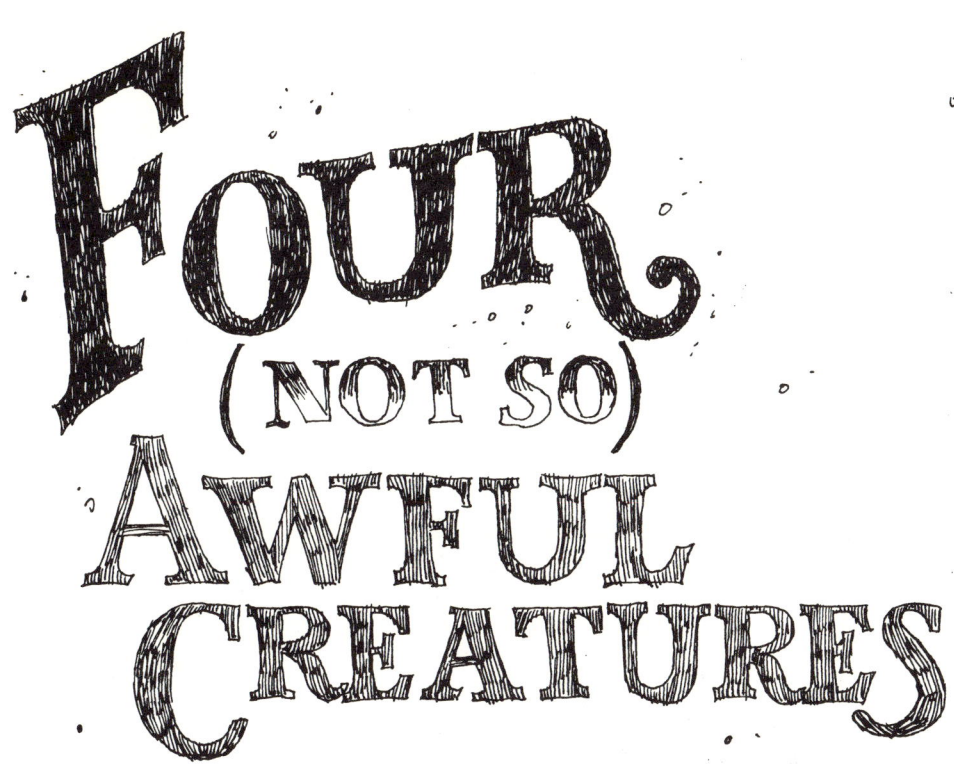

Four (NOT SO) Awful Creatures

BATS
SPIDERS
WOLVES
ALLIGATORS

Yucchh!!

A LARGE
BUT HARMLESS
TARANTULA

HARMLESS GARDEN SPIDER

Spiders! Many people say "Yucchh" when they see a picture of one.

This is what they say when they see a *real* one:

She: OH MY GOSH!! THERE—RIGHT THERE . . .!!

He:　A SPIDER!!! OH MY GOSH!!! IS IT ALIVE?!!

She: OF COURSE IT'S ALIVE!! ICCCH!! LOOK AT IT MOVE!! IT'S GOING TO BITE US!!

He:　KILL IT! KILL IT BEFORE IT BITES! KILL IT NOW!! YUCCCCHH!!

And so it goes. Another completely harmless spider is mashed to death.

HOW DANGEROUS ARE SPIDERS?

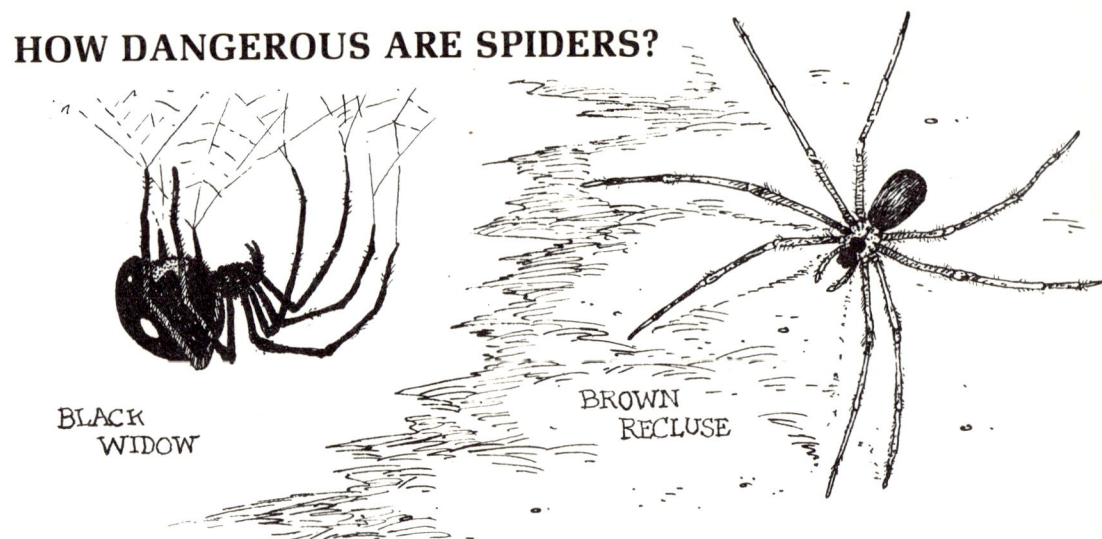

BLACK WIDOW

BROWN RECLUSE

There are about 2,000 different kinds of spiders in the United States and Canada. Of these, only *two* are known to be really dangerous. Only one kills—the black widow spider.

The black widow got its name because the female spider often eats the male, which is smaller. It is also known as the hour-glass spider because its body has a mark the shape of an hour-glass on it.

Black widow spiders are found all over the world. In North America, they are found everywhere but Alaska and northern Canada.

The bite of a black widow spider can kill. But only about one bite in twenty-five causes death. The person who is bitten usually gets over the sickness caused by the bite. The U.S. government says that in an average year seven people are killed in the United States by black widow bites.

A REAL CASE

This is a true case of a black widow bite.

A three-year-old girl was playing in a garage next to her home. Suddenly she cried out to her mother to come and get a bug off her neck.

The girl's mother came and found a black spider in her hair. She also found two small marks on her neck.

The mother killed the spider. She rushed the child to a doctor. The doctor saw that the dead spider was a black widow.

By now, the little girl was in pain. She said that both her stomach and her head hurt. She found it hard to breathe. She got sick and vomited.

Within a few minutes, the outside of her stomach became very hard. It became as hard as a board. She had very bad cramps.

These were all the signs of the bite of the black widow spider.

The doctor placed an ice pack over the two tiny wounds in her neck. He did this to lessen her pain. He put her to bed. He gave her some medicine to fight the poison. The little girl vomited over and over again.

But six hours later she seemed to be all right. She was all right the next day too. So the doctor let her go home.

The little girl's life was saved probably because her mother had acted so quickly. She was saved too because the doctor knew right away that the bug that bit her was a black widow spider.

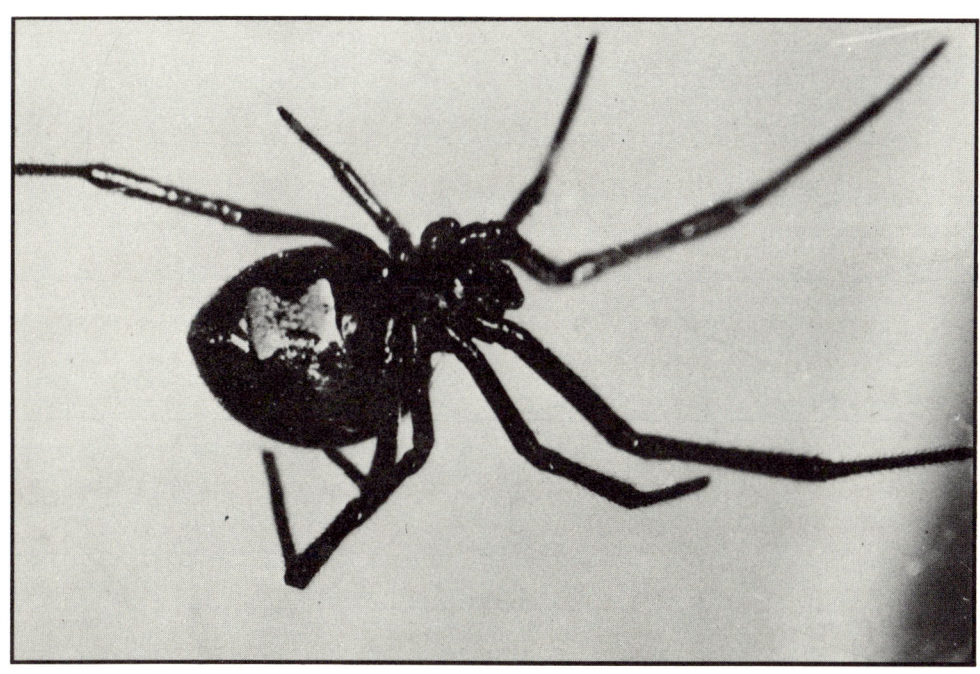

THE BROWN RECLUSE

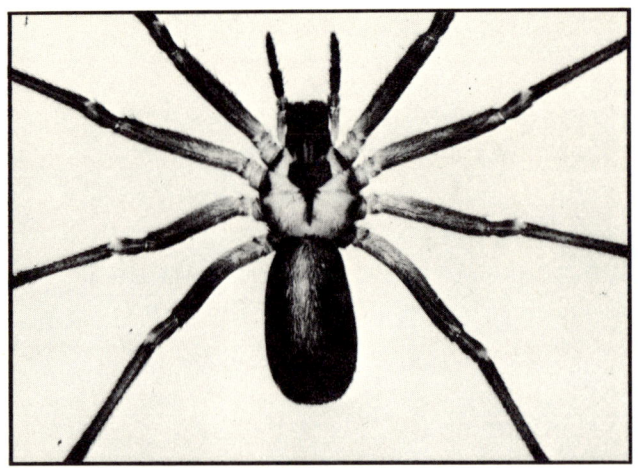

Another dangerous spider is the brown recluse or "fiddleback" spider. *Fiddle* is another word for *violin*. The fiddleback spider gets its name from the violin shape on the back of its head.

The brown recluse is found in the southern United States. Its poisonous relatives, the brown spiders, live in South America. Brown recluse bites almost never kill, but they do cause a lot of pain—and do a lot of damage to the skin. The poison of the brown recluse spider eats away at skin tissue.

Let's say a brown recluse bites a person on the finger. It may take a week or two, but, little by little, a deep hole forms where the bite was made. Those who are bitten get sick. They are in pain and have to stay in bed. They almost always get better, but the scars of the bites stay on their bodies.

YUCCCCHH!! The black widow and the brown recluse . . . two spiders to stay away from. Two kinds of spiders that really are dangerous. But they are only two ... two out of 2,000.

WHAT ABOUT THE OTHER 1,998?

All spiders have some poison in their bodies. All of them can bite. But none of them can do any serious damage to people.

Even the biggest of spiders, the great hairy tarantula, isn't really dangerous. In real life, it's pretty harmless. Only in stories and movies does it kill.

The bite of the tarantula feels like a pin prick. And it does about as much damage.

There *are* some dangerous tarantulas in South America. But there are no dangerous tarantulas in the United States.

In Fact . . .

Spiders don't even like to bite people. They are very shy, frightened creatures. When a person comes near, they think only of escape.

John Henry Comstock made the study of spiders his life's work. In his book *The Spider Book* Comstock wrote:

During my study of spiders I have collected thousands . . . and have taken very many in my hand but have never been bitten by one.

Once you come to know that most spiders you see are not dangerous, you can start to enjoy them. It's best not to handle spiders. But they are fun to watch. Spiders are interesting and unusual creatures.

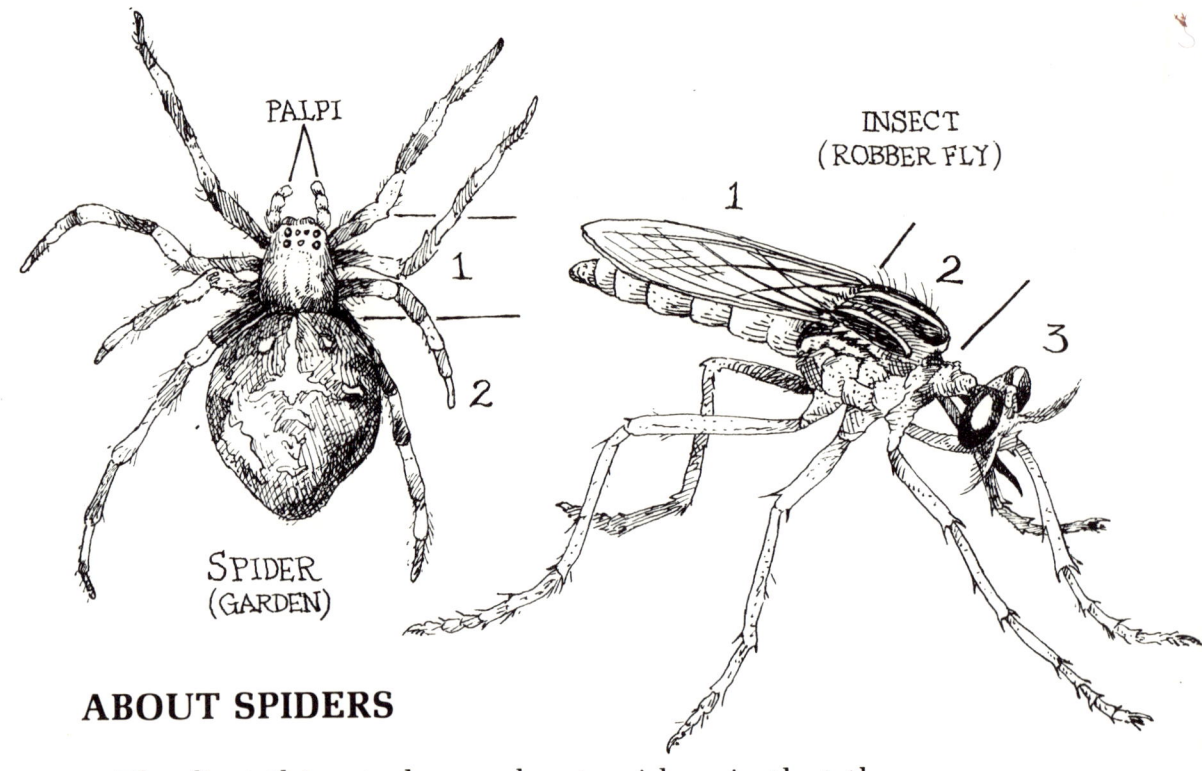

PALPI

INSECT
(ROBBER FLY)

1

2

1

2

3

SPIDER
(GARDEN)

ABOUT SPIDERS

The first thing to learn about spiders is that they are not insects. They may look like insects, but there are differences.

- All insects have six legs.
- All spiders have eight legs.
- The bodies of all insects can be divided into three parts.
- The bodies of all spiders can be divided into only two parts.

If spiders aren't insects, then what are they? Spiders are *arachnids*. Arachnids, unlike insects,

- have eight legs (instead of six).
- do not have wings.
- have a pair of feelers in front called *palpi*. They look like little legs, but are not for walking. Male spiders use palpi for mating.

WHAT SPIDERS EAT

The main food of spiders is insects. But spiders also eat other spiders. Very often, female spiders eat male spiders. The females are much larger and stronger than the males. Some large spiders eat tadpoles and even small birds.

Spiders don't really *eat* their food. They drink it. When a spider kills an insect, it puts *enzymes* into its prey's body. The enzymes are chemicals that turn the insides of the insect into liquid. The spider sucks out this liquid. When the spider finishes drinking, only the wings and the hard outside part of the insect's body are left.

Spiders eat a lot of food. But one of the most unusual things about them is that they can go a very long time without eating at all. Some small spiders can live well over a year without food!

14

HOW SPIDERS CATCH THEIR FOOD

"Come into my parlor," said the spider to the fly.

If you were a fly (or any other insect), you wouldn't want to go into a spider's parlor. You'd never come out again. For many spiders, their "parlor," or home, is their web. This is where they live—where they rest and wait for insects to show up and get caught and eaten. When danger comes, they run from the web.

Not all spiders live on their webs. Some live in nests nearby. Often, the nest is made of leaves. A thick thread runs from the web to the nest next door.

Here's how a spider catches food on its web:

1. An insect flies by mistake into the web. It gets caught on the sticky threads of the web. The lines that run across the web are coated with drops of a very sticky sort of gum.

2. The insect tries very hard to get free. It pulls and pushes to get away.

3. The insect's efforts make the web shake. They also make the thick thread that runs from the web to the spider's nest jump up and down.

4. Inside the nest, the spider is resting with its legs on the thread. It can feel the thread jump.

5. The spider runs out of the nest. It runs across the web. (An oil on the spider's body keeps it from getting caught on the web.)

6. The spider runs to the trapped insect and bites it. The insect's body is filled with poison from the spider.

7. When the insect is dead, the spider wraps its body up in silk.

8. The spider leaves the wrapped up insect on the web (like a snack in the refrigerator) until it's ready to eat it. There may be more than one insect wrapped up like this on the web.

9. The spider goes back to its nest to wait for another insect to get caught on the web.

CAUGHT IN THE WEB

WRAPPING THE PREY

WRAPPED AND IN STORAGE

WEBS

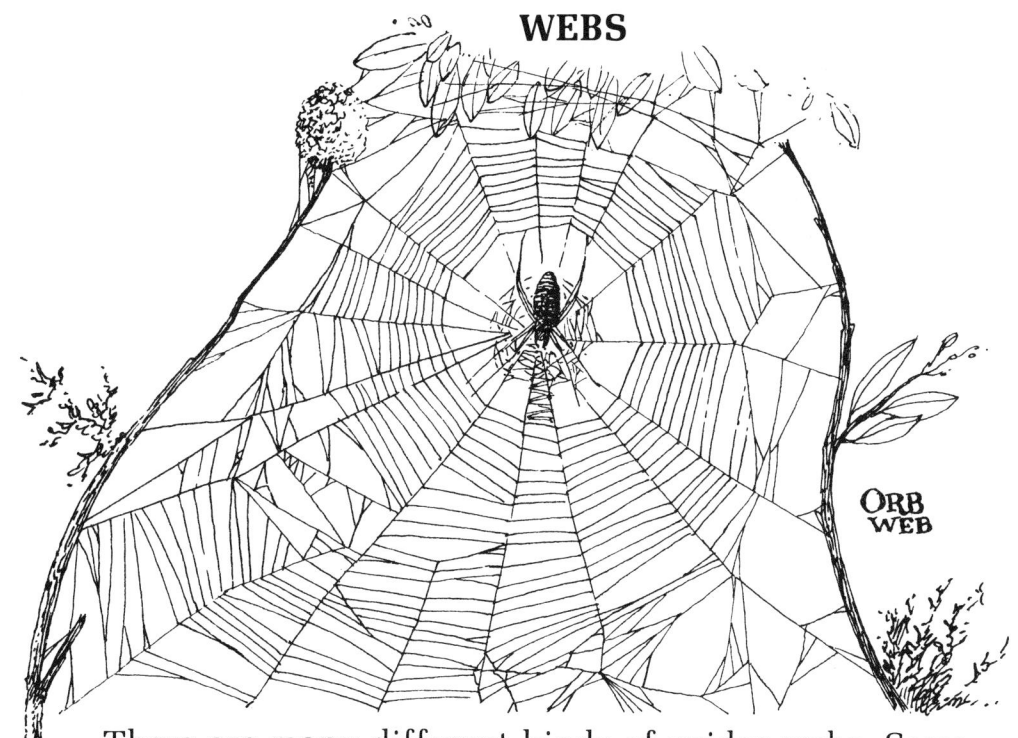

ORB WEB

There are many different kinds of spider webs. Some of the most beautiful webs are orb webs. They're made by garden spiders.

Spiders build their webs with silk. Silk is a very important part of the spider's world.

The silk comes from the spider. Inside its body, the spider makes wet, stringy material. The spider then draws a line of silk out of its body. It does this with the claws on its legs.

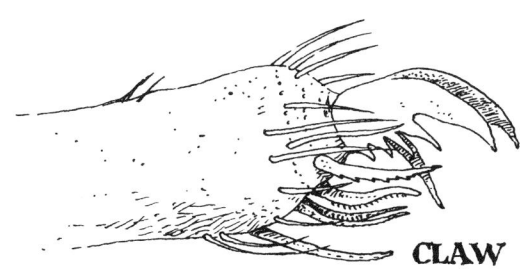

CLAW

Spiders use the claws on their legs to work with silk the way humans use their hands and fingers to work with other materials.

Spiders build webs with silk the way humans build bridges with steel.

Engineers, people who build things, really think a lot of the spider. They think the spider is a very fine natural engineer.

It's a fact that spiders were building suspension bridges millions of years before any human builder thought of building them.

The way a spider begins to build its orb web is the same way human builders begin to build a suspension bridge.

SUSPENSION
BRIDGE
(with bridge)
cables
only

STEPS IN BUILDING AN ORB WEB

First, the spider builds a bridge between two twigs. It makes the bridge stronger by walking back and forth over it. The spider lays down more silk as it walks.

Next, the spider builds a triangle of silk and attaches the bottom of it to a lower twig.

From there, the web takes off . . .

OTHER TYPES OF WEBS

The Funnel Web. Funnel webs are often found in houses. The funnel web has a wide sheet. At the corner of the sheet is a long narrow tube. *Funnel* is another word for *tube*. The spider lives inside this tube.

Above the wide sheet is a mixed-up bunch of silk threads. These threads are not sticky.

When an insect flies into them by mistake, it gets tripped up. It falls into the sheet below.

The house spider then darts from its tube, and catches the insect before it can get away.

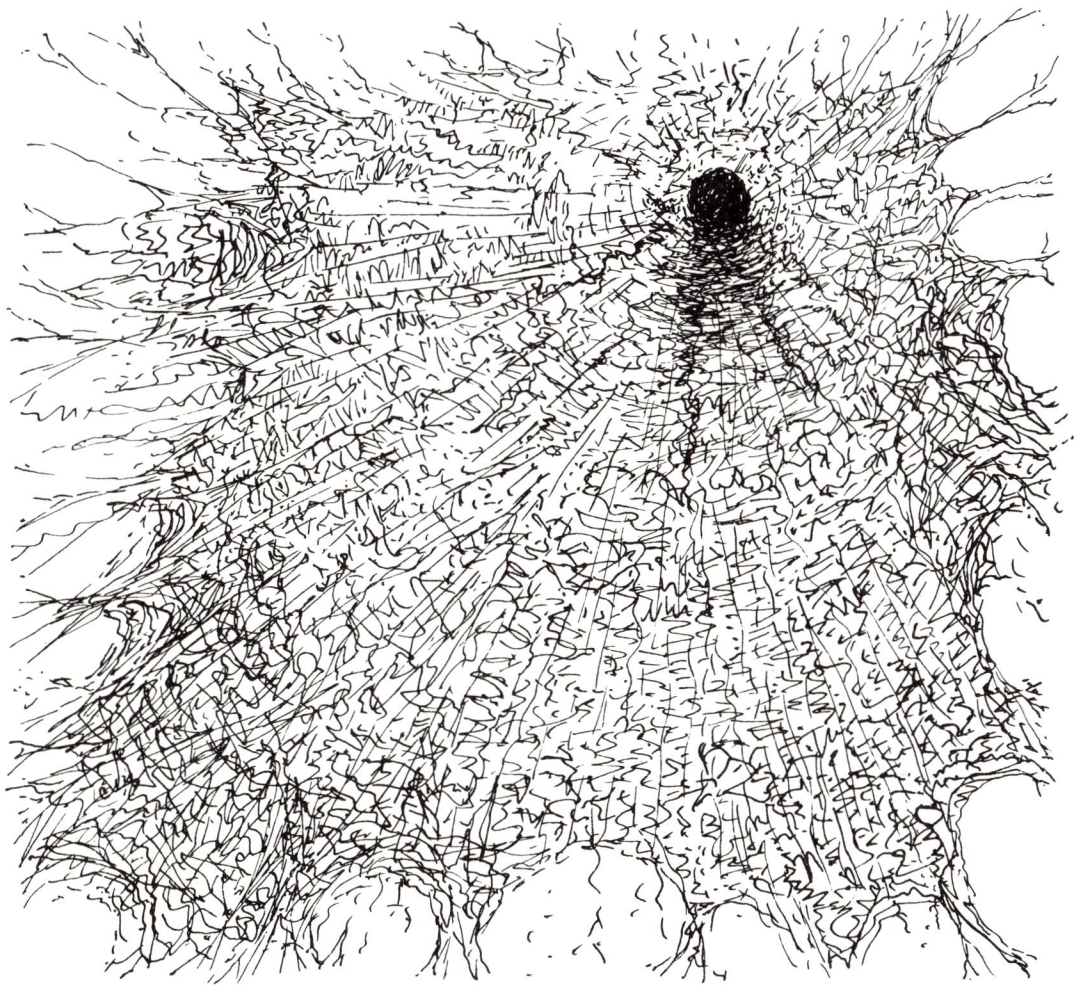

WEBS UNDER WATER

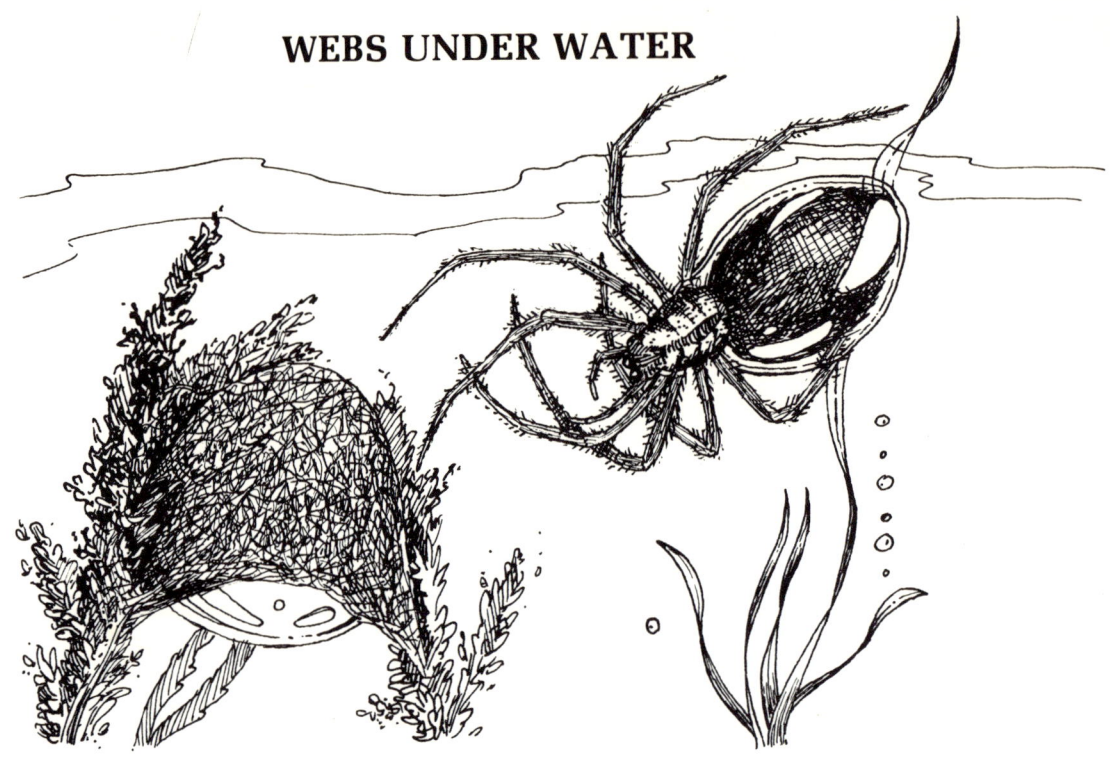

Spiders, like people, are air-breathing creatures. They need air to breathe.

But the water spider lives under water!

How does it do it?

As the water spider dives under water, it carries over its body a silvery bubble of air. The air bubble gives the spider air to breathe while it's under water.

The water spider spins a bell-shaped web for itself under water. This is usually tied down to a water weed.

The web is filled with air in a very clever, almost unbelievable way. The spider picks up an extra large bubble of air with its hind legs. It carries it down to the web, its new underwater home.

It does this over and over again until the web is completely filled with air.

Then it moves in and starts living in the web. It swims out from time to time to catch insects that live on top of the water. It even catches baby fish.

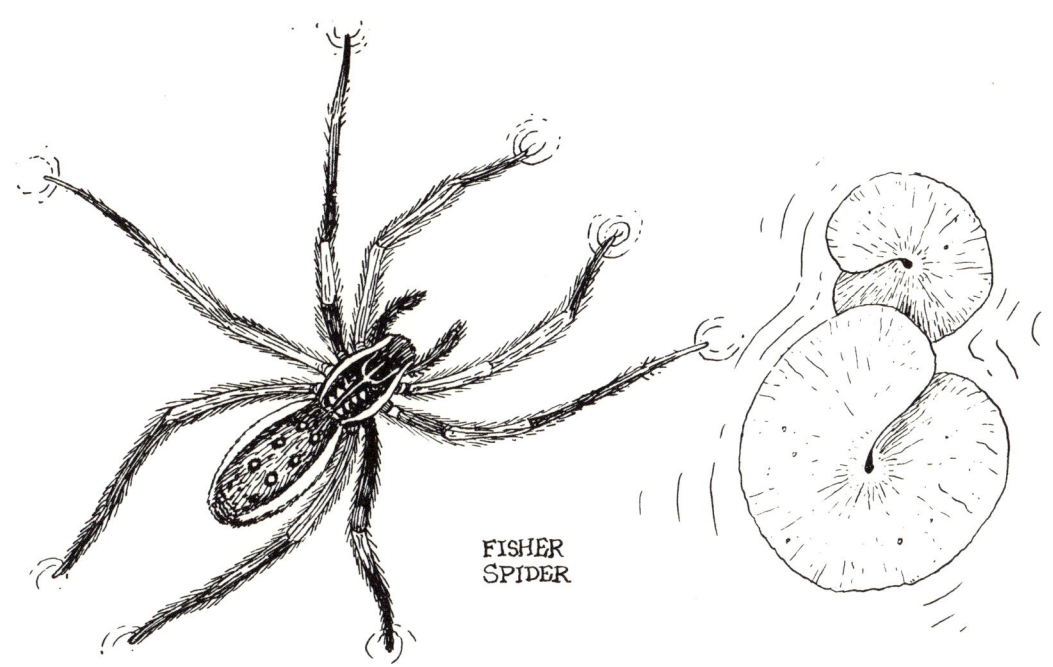

FISHER
SPIDER

Fisher Spiders don't live under water. They live on plants over water. They don't actually swim, but they can walk on the water easily. They catch mostly insects that live near the water, and also small fish.

The Raft Spider lives in swamps and streams in England. It was once believed that this spider made a tiny raft for itself out of silk and dead leaves. But it really doesn't do this. The raft spider is just a type of fisher spider that lives on plants by the water.

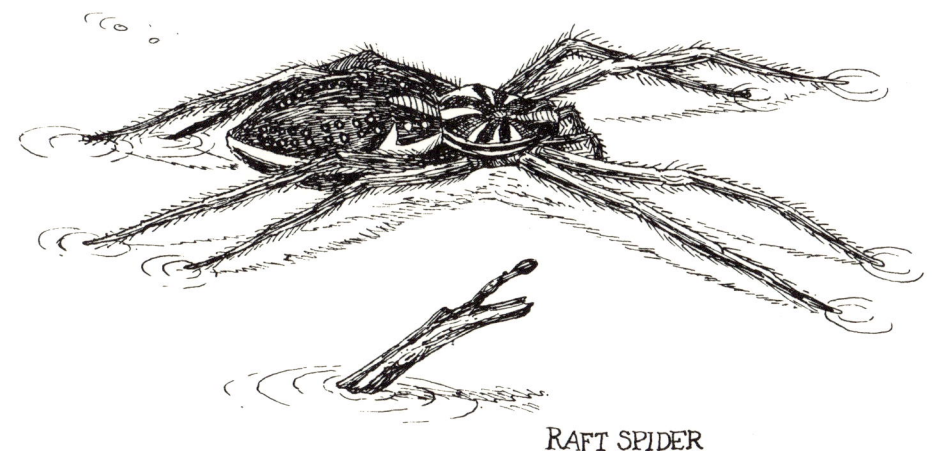

RAFT SPIDER

SPIDERS THAT HUNT

Not all spiders use webs to catch the insects they eat.
Some, such as wolf spiders, do their hunting—as wolves do—
on the ground.

Some of these hunting spiders have no homes at all. They
just wander around. They hunt by day, and spend the
night under a stone or any shelter they can find.

Others have homes. They live in holes in the ground.
And they spend most of their time standing at the entrances
looking out for passing insects.

Wolf spiders chase insects, and catch them on the ground.

WOLF SPIDER

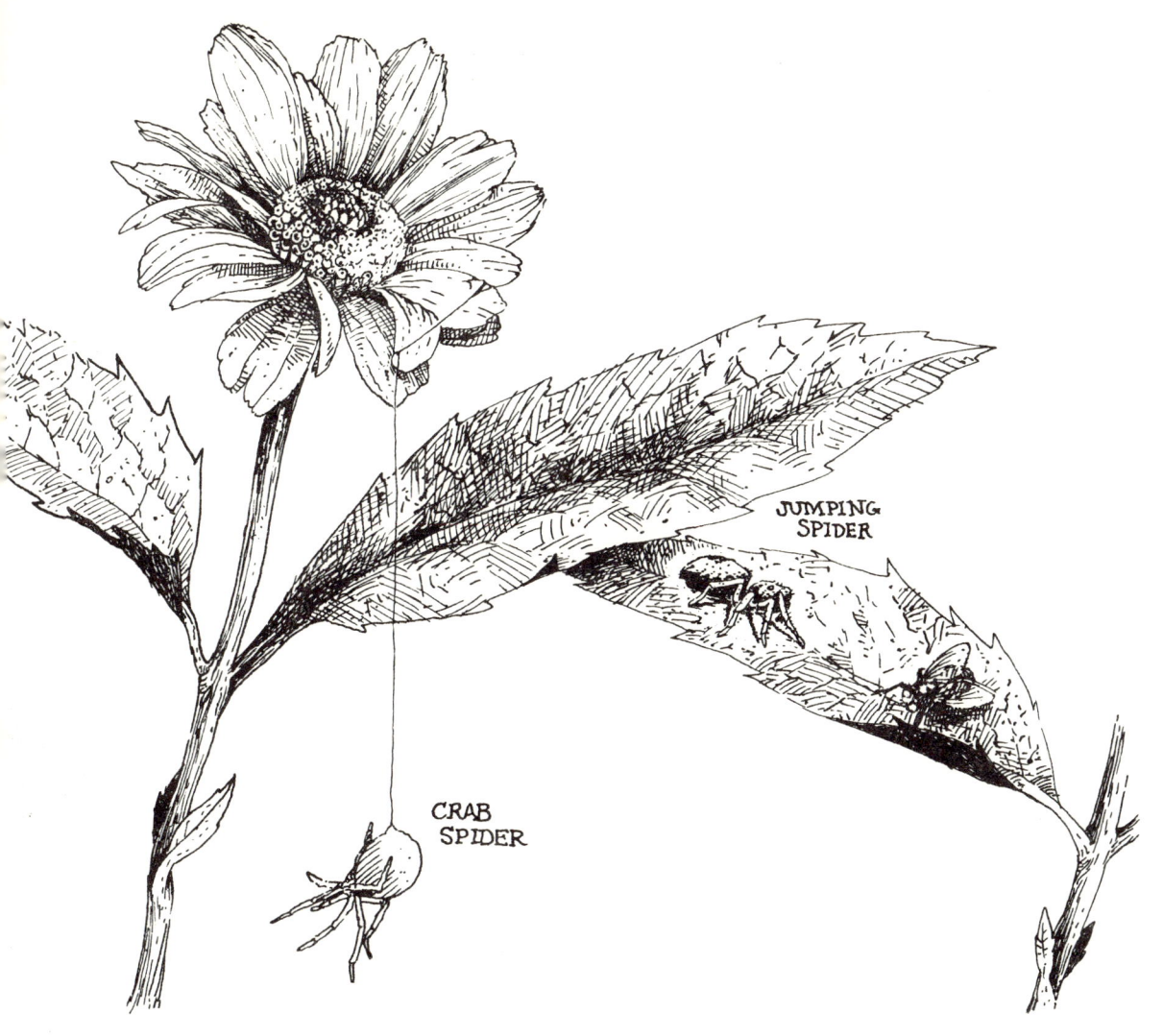

Jumping spiders have very large eyes and good eyesight. They creep up on flies the way cats creep up on mice. Jumping spiders may often be seen on walls and on the sides of houses.

Crab spiders usually hide out in flowers and plants. They can't be easily seen there.

Some crab spiders can change their color to match the color of the flower on which they're hiding. This makes it even harder to see them.

An insect visits a flower to suck some nectar. The hidden crab spider grabs it, and has itself a meal.

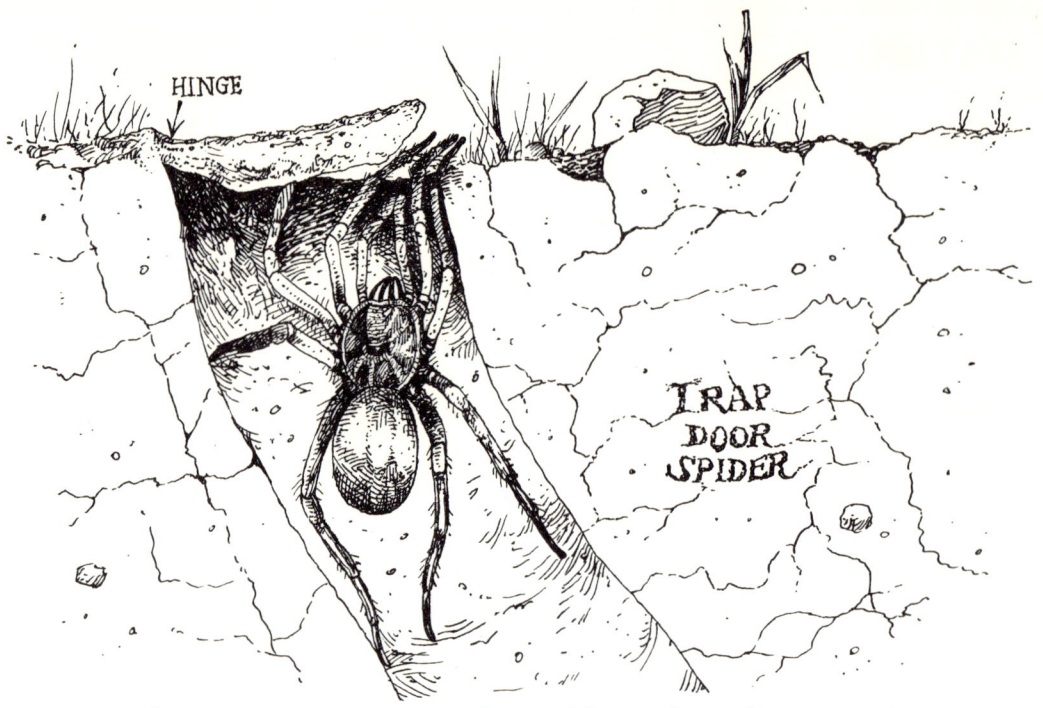

HINGE

TRAP DOOR SPIDER

Tarantulas, too, are among the spiders that do not spin webs, but hunt their prey on the ground. Tarantulas live in burrows.

There is a certain kind of tarantula that's known as the trap-door spider. It lives in the southern and western states. The trap-door spider is the inventor of something else engineers use quite a lot—the hinge. The homes of trap-door spiders had front doors that opened and shut long before people thought of the idea.

The trap-door spider coats the walls of its burrow with spit and earth. It makes them smooth, firm, and waterproof. Then it lines them with silk. The spider cuts a door in the earth above the burrow and lines it with silk too. By continuing the silk that lines the burrow into the silk that covers the door, the spider makes a hinge!

The trap-door spider can hold its front door closed against enemies. When it's ready to go hunting, it pushes the door open, and sits quietly until it can catch a grasshopper, a beetle, or other prey. Trap-door spiders usually stay pretty close to their burrows.

MATTING

When a male spider reaches maturity, he leaves his web and goes off into the world to find himself a mate.

This can be risky. Female spiders are much larger and stronger than males—and they sometimes eat them. But the male spider searches for a female anyway.

He goes to a female's web. He has a special way of letting her know he's around. He doesn't want her to mistake him for an insect. If he simply lands on the web, the female may just charge out, bite him, and eat him.

So he taps on the web in a special way. He taps a sort of Morse code message. It tells her simply that he is *not* an insect. He is a male who wishes to mate with her.

The female comes out, and the two spiders mate.

Some male spiders stay around after mating, and live with the female in the web.

Others, after mating, get away from the female as fast as their eight legs can carry them. This is often a good idea. Female spiders sometimes *do* eat males right after mating.

Many people believe that the female *always* kills the male right after mating. This is not true.

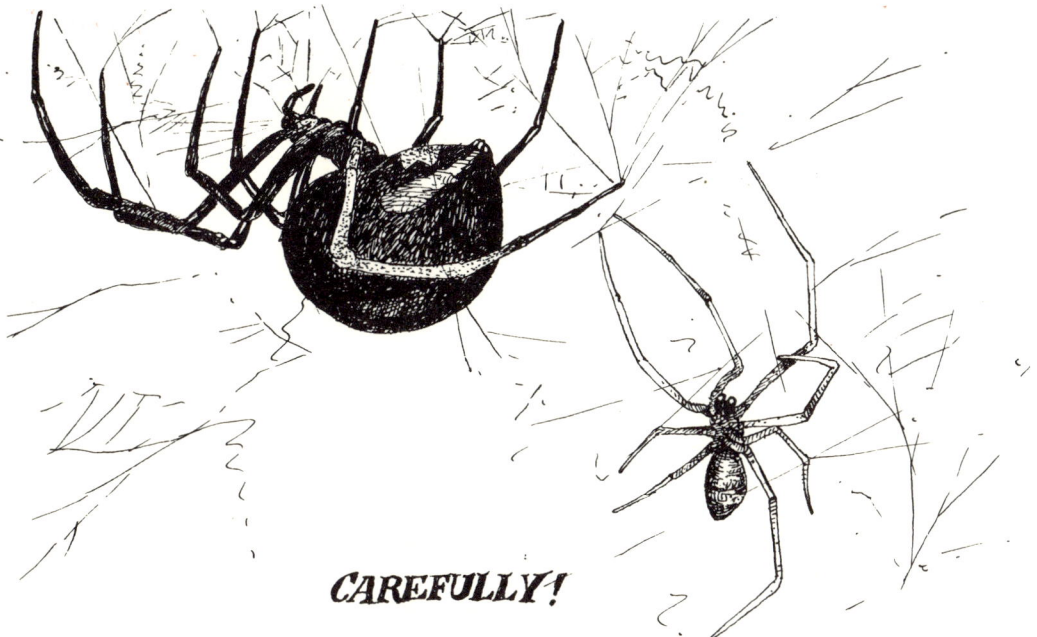

CAREFULLY!

27

Male wolf spiders and jumping spiders put on a show for females they want to mate with.

The male puts on a dance for the female. He may jump up and down or from side to side, waving his legs and palpi at the female.

The male nursery web spider gives a present to the female he wants to mate with. He catches an insect, wraps it in silk, and gives it to the female, just as human males present their dates with flowers or boxes of candy.

Crab spiders have odd mating habits. In one species, the male ties his wife to the ground with silk threads. He does this to keep her from eating him.

Whether he gets eaten or not, the male spider often dies soon after mating.

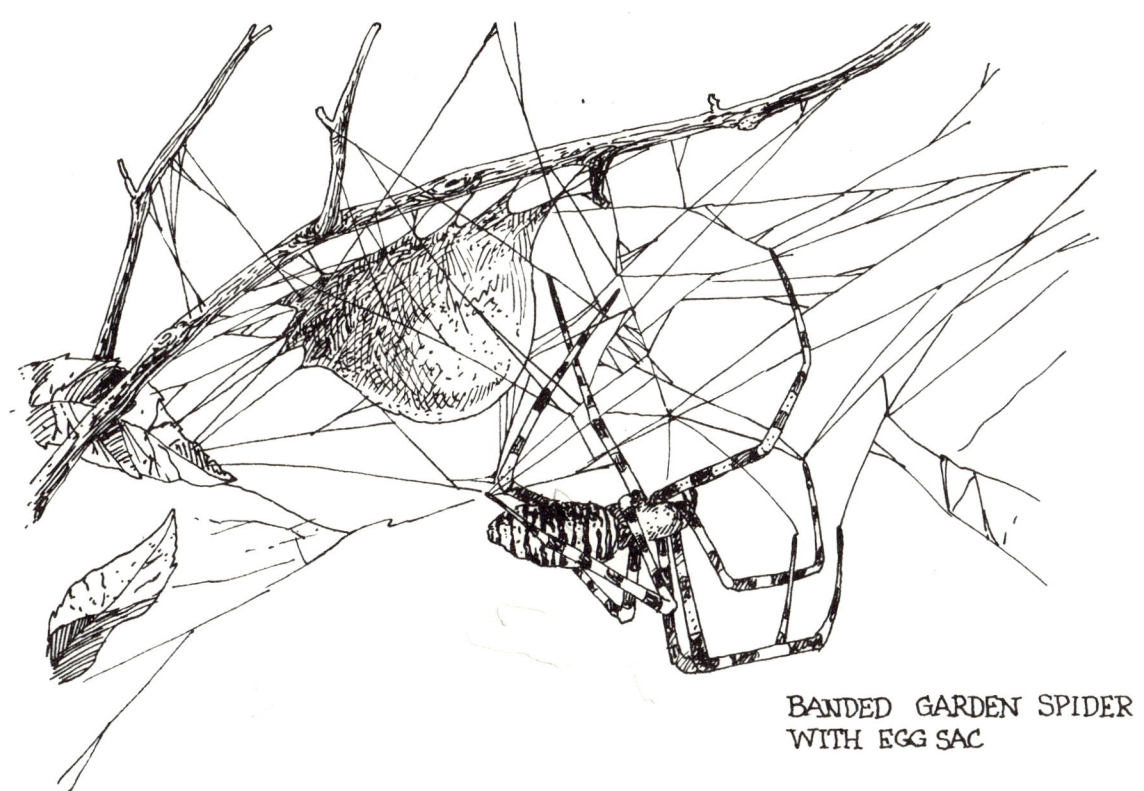

BANDED GARDEN SPIDER
WITH EGG SAC

SPIDER MOTHERS

The garden spider mother lays her eggs on a dish of silk. Then she covers them with still more silk. The silk forms a sac, or *cocoon,* and protects the eggs.

The cocoon is hidden among plants so that enemies such as wasps can't find it and break into it.

The female garden spider dies soon after making a cocoon. She doesn't live to see her babies born.

In time the eggs hatch, and the baby spiders, called *spiderlings,* are born. Right away—without a mother—they are on their own. Soon they are building their own webs.

Spiderlings grow by *molting.* This means that, as they grow, they break out of their old, tight skin. There's a new, soft skin underneath that will fit the spiderling for a while.

They do this eight or nine times before they are fully grown.

NURSERY WEB
SPIDER
WITH EGG SAC

In some species of spiders, the mother makes her cocoon on the web. After the babies hatch, the mother and her children live together for a long while on the same web.

The nursery web spider carries her egg sac around with her under her body wherever she goes. This is very hard for her. The egg sac is so large that the mother has to run on the tips of her legs to keep it from dragging on the ground. She only lets the sac touch the ground when she rests.

When the spiderlings are about to be born, the mother goes to a plant. She places the egg sac on the top of the plant. Then she ties it down to the plant by spinning a web over the leaves.

She then stands guard next to it until her babies are born.

Wolf spiders also carry their egg sac around with them while they go hunting for food. They drag it along behind them.

For quite a while after the babies are born, the wolf spider mother carries them around on her back.

WOLF SPIDER
WITH BABIES

DO SPIDERS FLY?

Spiders don't have wings. And yet, they do fly. They sail through the air—sometimes for hundreds of miles. This is something people have in common with spiders. Neither of us has wings, and yet we both manage to fly.

How do spiders do it? They do it the way they do almost everything else—with the aid of silk.

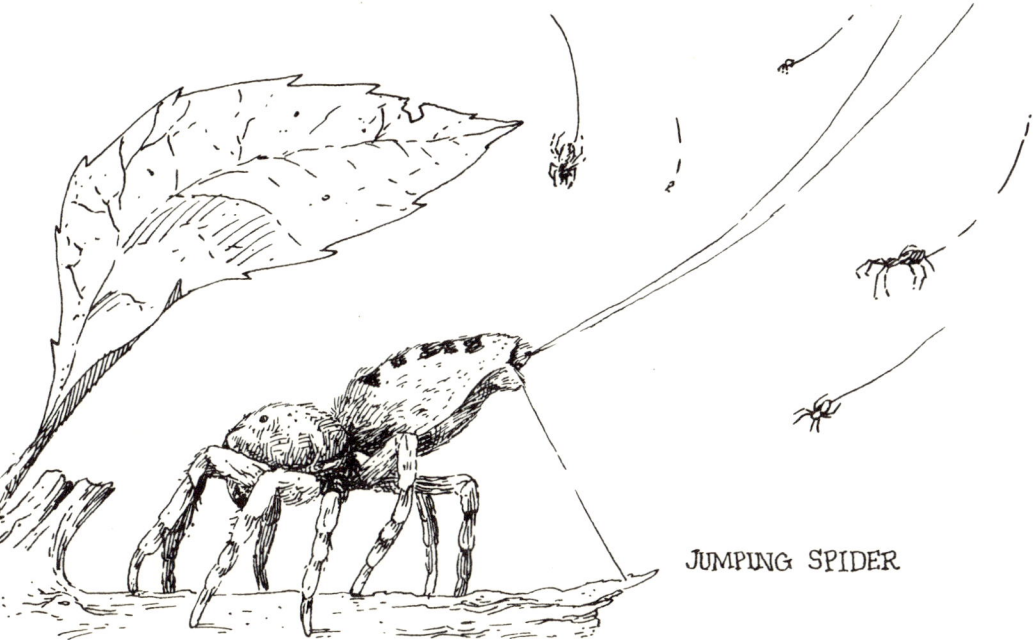

JUMPING SPIDER

It's mostly very young spiderlings that fly. In the spring and fall, the air is filled with millions of flying spiderlings.

A spiderling makes its way to a high point on a plant or a fence.

It faces into a breeze. It stretches out its legs and tilts up its abdomen.

Silk threads are drawn from the body by puffs of air. The threads keep streaming out.

Then the little spider lets itself fly. Off it goes. The puffs of air and the silk threads pull it up into space. The silk threads act the way a balloon does.

The little spider can fly up to about 200 feet over the earth.

The little spider may not fly far at all—perhaps only a few yards. But spiderlings have been seen landing on ships hundreds of miles at sea.

There is a good reason why spiderlings fly. A mother spider may give birth to many babies at one time. If they all stayed in the same spot, there wouldn't be enough food or room for all of them. And so, it's important that they scatter and spread themselves out over the land.

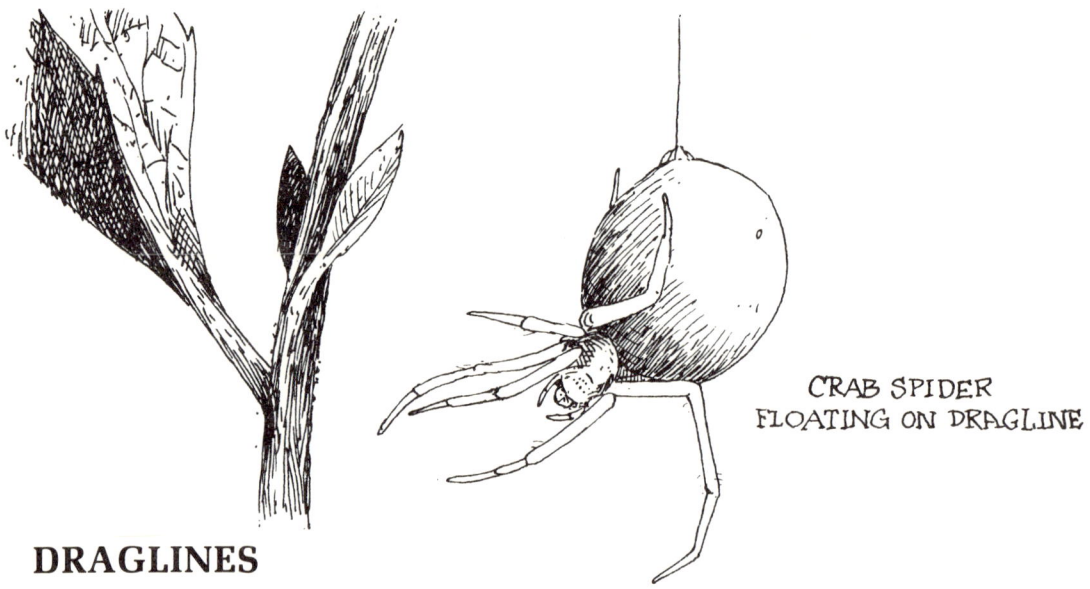

CRAB SPIDER
FLOATING ON DRAGLINE

DRAGLINES

Even on the ground, a spider usually has a thread of silk trailing along behind it. This is called the spider's *dragline.* The dragline helps the spider to know where it is. When it wanders away from home, it can follow the dragline back to where it came from.

Often, it acts as the spider's "life line." Many times, it actually saves the little creature's life.

A spider is resting in the web. Along comes an enemy. By means of the dragline, the spider can make a quick drop, and then hide out in the grass until the enemy goes away.

With a dragline, a spider can leap from a building, a cliff, or any high place without getting hurt. It doesn't fall; it just floats smoothly down on the dragline.

ENEMIES OF SPIDERS

DIGGER WASP

The lives of spiders are filled with danger.

A mother spider may lay one hundred eggs. But only one or two spiderlings may live long enough to become full-grown spiders. Many are eaten by birds, frogs, and lizards. More are killed by certain kinds of wasps.

The wasps lay their eggs on the backs of young and adult spiders. The eggs hatch into grubs. The grubs hang on, and feed on the living spiders' bodies until they kill them.

The worst death of all comes from the digger wasp.

The wasp stings the spider. But the spider isn't killed. The sting makes it impossible for the spider to move.

The wasp then places the helpless spider inside a cell, and lays an egg on the spider's body.

When the wasp egg hatches, a grub comes out. The young grub eats the helpless spider little by little. The spider can't even move, let alone try to get away.

Many spiders are eaten by other spiders. All through their lives, spiders live in fear of being eaten by their own kind.

Even if spiders are not killed, most live less than a year. They are born in the spring, grow up during the summer, become adults in early autumn, mate, lay their eggs, and die before winter. But some larger spiders live as long as five years. And great tarantulas and trap-door spiders may live as long as fifteen, twenty, or even twenty-five years.

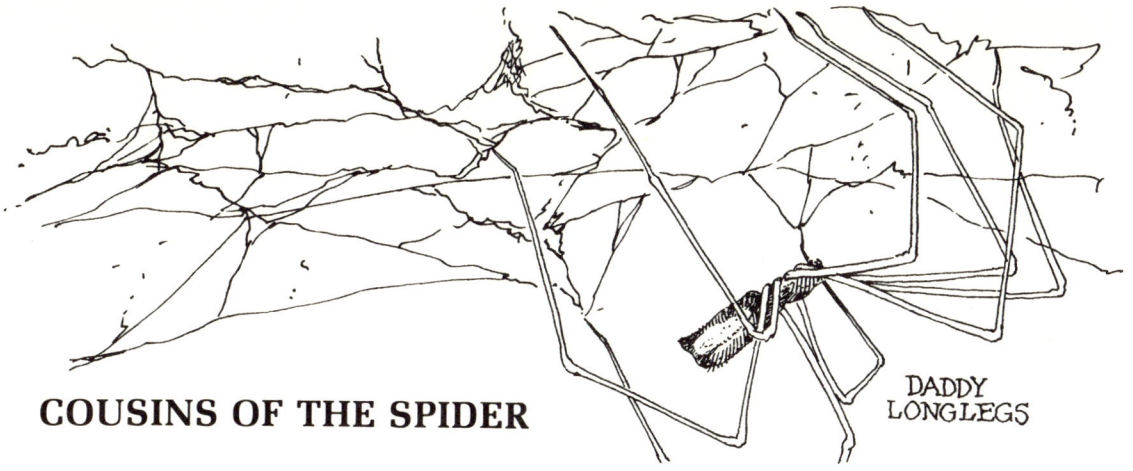

DADDY
LONGLEGS

COUSINS OF THE SPIDER

Daddy longlegs and scorpions are closely related to the spider. They are *arachnids*, though not true spiders.

You can tell a daddy longlegs by its very long, thin legs. If one of its legs gets caught, a daddy longlegs will shed the leg and try to escape. Daddy longlegs are also called harvestmen because they are most often seen during harvest time.

The daddy longlegs is harmless to people.

Scorpions *aren't* so harmless. The scorpion is easy to pick out because it looks so much like a crab.

Scorpions like warm climates. They are quite common in Mexico and Arizona.

All scorpion stings are believed to be dangerous. The bites of two types of scorpions found in southern Arizona are particularly harmful. Only about one scorpion bite in four hundred ends in death. But it's wise to keep away from scorpions.

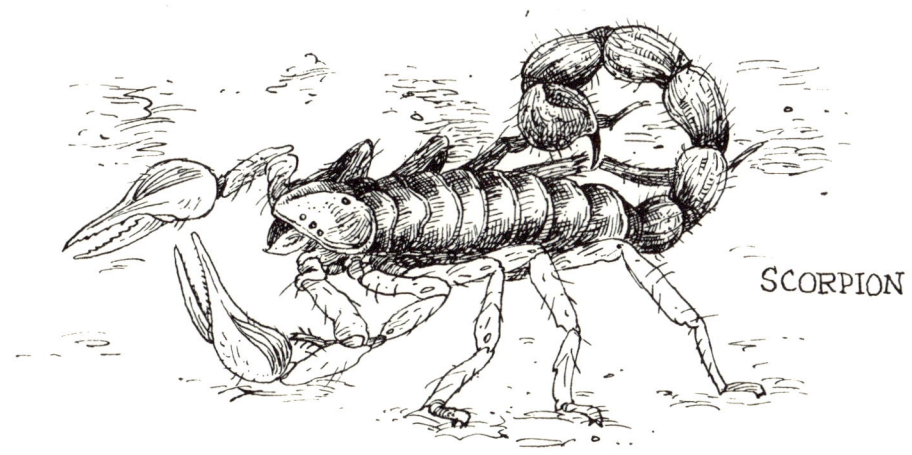

SCORPION

LOOKING FOR A REASON TO LIKE SPIDERS?

Spiders do people a lot of good. It's believed that if it weren't for spiders, all living creatures (except caterpillars) might starve. There would simply be very little left to eat. Insects would eat most of it. Every year, spiders kill billions and billions of harmful insects that ruin crops and spread disease.

Several ways have been used to get rid of harmful, plant-eating insects. One way was a chemical poison called DDT.

DDT worked very well. It seemed to be a great way to kill billions and billions of harmful insects. For many years, great clouds of the stuff were sprayed on crops. People were very happy with the way it worked.

Then, little by little, people found out the truth about DDT. Not only was it killing harmful insects; it was killing other life for miles around. The poison had a way of spreading far and wide. And its effects lasted for a long time. Animals, birds, even fish were dying in many different places.

By the late 1960s, DDT was being used less and less. Now it is hardly used at all.

Much damage was done. But people learned a great lesson. We learned that we have to be very careful about the way we get rid of harmful insects. Chemical poisons are still used. But they are not nearly as dangerous as DDT.

Spiders are a very good and completely safe way of getting rid of insects that eat crops. They've been doing it for millions of years, and haven't done any harm yet.

A single acre of land may have as many as two million spiders. Every day, a spider eats an average of three times its own weight. That's a lot of insects.

Spiders are among the best friends people have.

DID YOU KNOW?

- In 17th century England, people sometimes ate spider sandwiches as a cure for certain illnesses. They took dozens of little spiders, mashed them up, and spread them on bread the way we smear on butter. (Doctors no longer favor spider sandwiches as a cure for anything).

- People in Italy during the Middle Ages claimed that the bite of the tarantula caused them to break out into wild dancing. There is still a dance in Italy called the *tarantella*. The tarantula got its name from the dance.

Spider sandwiches? And tarantulas that caused wild dancing?

There are a lot of ideas that people have had about spiders that just aren't true.

Maybe you've had some of these ideas yourself. Maybe you've had the one big idea that so many people have—that all spiders are dangerous.

We hope this book has made a difference. We hope that, because of it, you no longer see all spiders as enemies.

Most, of course, are not. Most actually do a great deal of good. They eat great numbers of harmful insects.

And they're interesting little creatures.

We hope that, perhaps because of this book, you may have even gotten to *like* spiders.

They're not so hard to like.

And the next time you see one perhaps you won't run from it or try to kill it.

Maybe you won't even say: "YUCCCCHHH!!!"

Unless, of course, someone offers you a spider sandwich!

INDEX